THIS BOOK IS FULL OF HOLES

For everyone who eagerly brainstormed
about holes with me, especially Sabina
and my grandmother Ruth

—N. N.

To my dad, who loved digging
around in the garden

—R. M.

Ω

Published by
PEACHTREE PUBLISHING COMPANY INC.
1700 Chattahoochee Avenue
Atlanta, Georgia 30318-2112
PeachtreeBooks.com

Text © 2024 by Nora Nickum
Illustrations © 2024 by Robert Meganck

Edited by Kathy Landwehr
Design and composition by Lily Steele
The illustrations were digitally rendered.

Printed and bound in November 2023 at Toppan Leefung, DongGuan, China.
10 9 8 7 6 5 4 3 2 1
First Edition
ISBN 978-1-68263-600-8

Cataloging-in-Publication Data is available from the Library of Congress.

THIS BOOK IS FULL OF HOLES

OF HOLES

From Underground to Outer Space and Everywhere In Between

Written by
Nora Nickum

Illustrated by
Robert Meganck

PEACHTREE
ATLANTA

What is a hole?

A hollow place.
An empty space.

A part of something
where there's
nothing at all.

But wait—there's **something**
to that **nothing.**

A hole can be beautiful.
Surprising. Useful.
Alarming!

So look around.
What holes do you see?

Maybe there's a hole on the shelf
where you plucked out this book.

Or some extra holes in your neighbor's nose.

There may be holes in your clothes that
make them wearable—or not so much.

You may spot a hole
made by an animal.

Or one created by
a builder or an artist,
a cook or an engineer.

The world of holes is big.

Let's dig in!

A hole can be an

indentation . . .

An indentation is a dent or a hollow place in something—a hole with a bottom. This kind of hole is useful if you want your syrup or honey to stay put, for example.

. . . or open.

An open hole doesn't have a bottom. That's helpful if you want something to pass right through it and come out the other side, like thread through the eye of a needle.

A hole can be found on land . . .

In 2014, helicopter pilots spotted a massive hole in the Siberian Arctic. It had been caused by a mysterious explosion that threw chunks of rock and ice for great distances, leaving behind a crater estimated to be 66 feet (20 meters) wide and 171 feet (52 meters) deep. Since then, additional craters have been discovered in the region. Scientists think they are caused by methane gas that builds up under ice and soil, making a mound and increasing the pressure until it ruptures. But they are still puzzling out where the gas comes from and why the pressure gets so high.

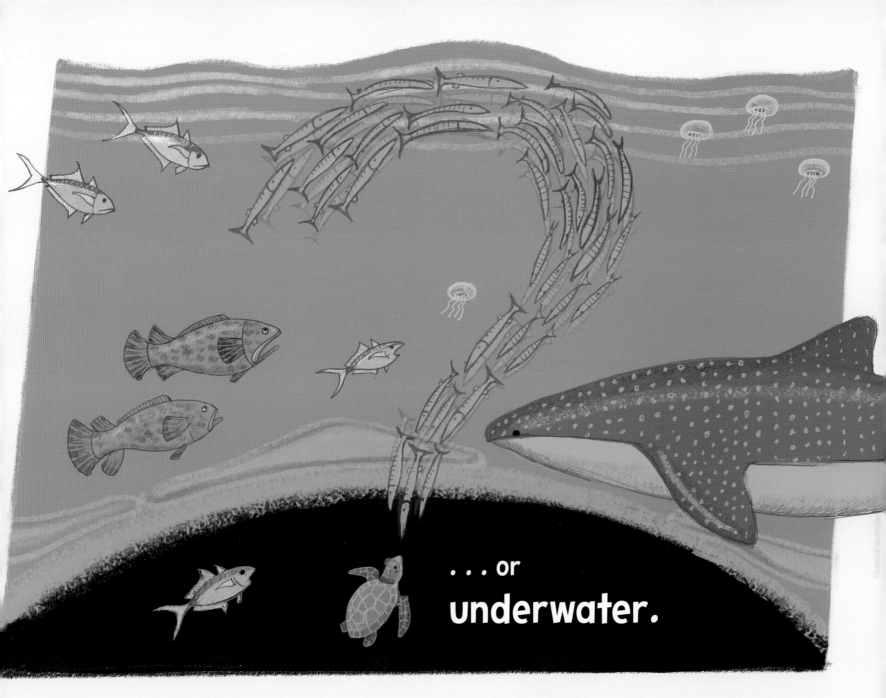

. . . or
underwater.

Some holes that originally formed on land are now located in the ocean. They didn't shuffle their way out to sea, though—the water came to them. About 15,000 years ago, ice sheets began to melt and sea levels rose, flooding some areas and filling caves and sinkholes with water. Ta-da! Blue holes. The water in a blue hole has less oxygen than the surrounding ocean. Scientists are studying how blue holes support marine life and what unique species of bacteria or invertebrates live there. One of the deepest known blue holes, near China, extends about 1,000 feet (305 meters) down into the surrounding ocean. Others are in places like the Caribbean and Red seas, and there are surely more that are still undiscovered.

A hole can be made by a human . . .

About 82,000 years ago, humans in present-day North Africa punched holes in shells. Today, the wear and shine on the inside of the holes indicates these shells may have been put on strings and worn as beads. Archaeologists study objects like these to learn when humans began to do things like wear symbolic adornments and develop shared culture. Bead-making seems to have appeared in Africa and Asia about 40,000 years before it began in Europe.

. . . or another **animal.**

A small round hole in an empty clamshell lying on the beach is actually a clue in a murder—and the body that was inside the shell is missing. Whodunnit? The prime suspect is a moon snail. The largest of these marine snails, Lewis's moon snail, can fill its foot with water until it's about 12 inches (30.5 centimeters) long and use it to move around. When the moon snail finds a clam, it grabs on with its foot, then drills a hole through the clamshell with its long, toothed tongue. It can take the moon snail a few days to finish the hole, even with the help of an acid it releases, which scientists think dissolves the clamshell and the creature inside. Then it slurps out its meal and leaves behind the evidence.

When you're riding in a car and it jolts over a pothole, you may complain. But just remember, cars like yours are part of why the pothole is there. It starts with water gradually seeping into cracks in the surface of the road. When the temperature drops, the water freezes and expands, weakening the pavement. In warm weather, the ice thaws and the water drains away, leaving a hole. As vehicles drive over it, they kick out loose pieces, and the pothole grows larger while the people bumping over it groan louder.

. . . or quickly.

Imagine arriving at the bus stop, only to find it's now located at the bottom of a giant hole. You might wonder if you still have to go to school. You might also wonder where the hole came from. If the ground is largely composed of limestone or salt, it can be dissolved by water, creating a hidden cavern under the surface. Over time, the ground above the cavern becomes thin and may collapse into what is known as a sinkhole. Sometimes this can occur in less than a day!

A hole can be
deep . . .

In 1970, drilling began in Russia on the deepest human-made hole, created to enable geologists to study the Earth's crust. At over 7.6 miles (12.3 kilometers) deep, the Kola Superdeep Borehole could have fit a stack of 2,000 giraffes, except it was only 9 inches (23 centimeters) wide. It would have been way too hot for giraffes, too, because of processes like the radioactive decay of uranium and potassium in Earth's crust and mantle. The team was surprised to find tiny plankton fossils 4 miles (6.4 kilometers) down that hadn't been destroyed by the heat. As they drilled deeper, it got too hot for their equipment—356 degrees Fahrenheit (180 degrees Celsius), a better fit for baking cookies—and in 1992, they called it quits.

. . . or
shallow.

A baby periodical cicada, known as a nymph, digs a hole about a foot (30 centimeters) deep into the dirt to dine on tree root sap until its seventeenth birthday. Then, when the weather gets warm, it emerges, along with millions of its friends. They leave behind tiny exit holes on their way to a raucous cicada party. For a few weeks, they make a boisterous buzz while they molt, mate, lay eggs, and die. Periodical broods are on different thirteen- or seventeen-year cycles. Swarms of cicadas will emerge from holes in the ground in the eastern United States in 2024, 2025, 2029, and beyond.

A hole can be tiny . . .

Engineers put a bleed hole in the middle pane of each airplane window to help make your flight uneventful. Without that tiny hole, which is typically smaller than a peppercorn, the difference in air pressure inside and outside the plane could cause the window to break. The hole also lets moisture escape so the window doesn't fog up and spoil your view.

...or

enormous.

Astronauts in the International Space Station, orbiting above Earth, can see the huge holes of open-pit mines where people dug up copper and gold. The Bingham Canyon Mine in Utah is the world's largest human-made excavation. At 2.75 miles (4.4 kilometers) long and 0.75 miles (1.2 kilometers) deep, it's as long as thirty-eight soccer fields and deeper than six Space Needles balanced on top of each other. To get the valuable minerals, operators drill narrow holes as deep as four-story buildings. When they drop in explosives, the blasts scatter loose rock that can be scooped right up.

There can be a lot of holes . . .

A sprinkler has many holes, so it can scatter water over a wide area. But as it sprays small drops upward, quite a bit of water will evaporate or blow away before it has a chance to refresh a plant's roots—or you.

. . . or just **one.**

A hose's single hole focuses water in just one spot, whether that's a birdbath or a friend who may or may not be ready for a soaking.

A hole can be left empty . . .

The leaves of a Swiss cheese plant are dotted with holes, but not because they've been chewed. These plants—various species of *Monstera* native to Mexico and Central America—live mostly shaded by rainforest trees. Computer simulations show that a large leaf with holes will catch more specks of sunlight than a somewhat smaller leaf with no holes can, and growing a leaf with holes requires less energy than growing an intact one.

. . . or filled.

For insects and other small animals, the hole in a pitcher plant is a deadly trap. The captive is drawn to the plant's nectar, but once it tumbles from the slippery rim, it won't have much luck escaping, given the plant's smooth sides, downward-pointing hairs, and pool of liquid at the bottom. The plant digests its prey, getting nutrients it wasn't able to get from the soil, and waits for the next meal to tumble down the hole.

A hole can be made
to get in ...

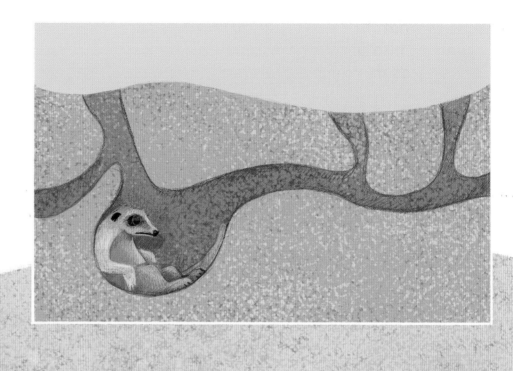

Mobs of meerkats move between several elaborate burrows, where they can stay cool and safe. They dig their own homes and also use those dug by other animals, like ground squirrels. They also make hundreds of smaller emergency boltholes all around their territory and remember where each one is located. (Don't challenge a meerkat to a game of memory!) If they're roaming in search of food and their lookout squeaks or barks at the sight of a predator, the group can dive into a bolthole and hide.

The holes that meerkats use to enter their burrows are also important escape routes. If a predator finds its way into their home, they can slip out a back door. Meerkats prefer to sleep in their larger burrows, perhaps because there are more exit holes.

. . . or OUT.

A hole can speed something up . . .

Engineers put lightening holes in parts of cars and airplanes. These holes make vehicles lighter so they can move faster and use less fuel. (Of course, there are places not to put these holes, like in the luggage hold or the fuel tank.)

. . . or **slow it down.**

The holes in a wiffle ball increase the air resistance so the ball can't move as fast or travel as far. That's good if you need to avoid hitting the ball into your neighbor's yard, but not so good if your team needs a home run to win the game.

A hole can make it possible to breathe . . .

A whale has a blowhole like a nostril on top of its head, which lets it breathe in and out without coming very far out of the water. Toothed whales like orcas have a single blowhole, while baleen whales like humpbacks get two.

. . . or beat the heat.

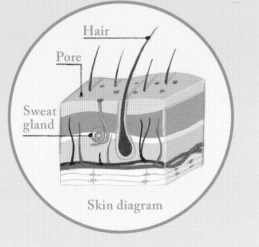

Hair

Pore

Sweat gland

Skin diagram

You have about three million pores in your skin, which keep your body from overheating when you're running a race (or just chasing after the ice-cream truck). They do that by releasing sweat, which takes away heat when it evaporates.

In the Arctic, a ringed seal hangs out under sea ice that can be several feet thick, hunting for fish and crustaceans. But it can't breathe underwater, so it uses the claws on its front flippers to make and maintain several breathing holes in the ice.

A hole can be a lifesaver . . .

. . . or pose a **danger**.

A polar bear may be waiting patiently at one of these holes. At mealtime, ringed seals are the main item on the polar bear's menu. When a seal needs to come up for air, it had better watch out!

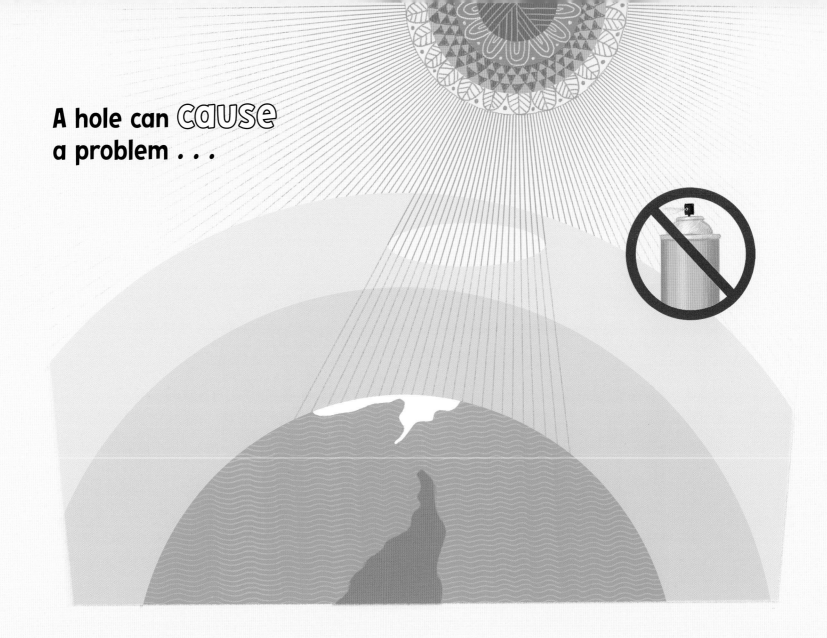

A hole can cause a problem . . .

In the 1980s, scientists discovered a hole in the ozone layer above Antarctica. Ozone is a gas found primarily in Earth's stratosphere—between 9 and 22 miles (15 and 35 kilometers) up. The ozone layer provides protection from the Sun's damaging ultraviolet radiation. But inventions like refrigerators, air conditioners, and spray cans used chlorine gases that drifted up and were converted into reactive gases by the Sun's radiation. Those gases destroyed ozone, creating the hole. For humans, that hole meant less protection and more skin cancer and cataracts. Uh-oh. In 1987, countries signed the Montreal Protocol—the first treaty to be ultimately joined by every country in the world—agreeing to be nicer to the ozone layer. They would stop making and using so much of the harmful gases that caused the hole. While a hole still appears every spring, it's shrinking because of those efforts. Whew! If countries follow through on their promises, scientists expect substantial recovery of the ozone layer around 2066.

. . . or solve one.

The unobtrusive holes along the top edge of your bathroom tub and sink will save the day if you ever plug the drain for a bubble bath and then forget to turn the water off. These overflow drains are designed to prevent the kind of disaster that'd turn your bathroom floor into a lake.

A hole can be used to make art . . .

Paper cutting has a rich, 1,500-year history in China (where paper was first invented). The artist creates an intricate, symbolic image by using a knife or scissors to cut holes in a single sheet of paper. The final piece may be used in celebrations or to decorate a door or window where the light can shine through.

. . . or music.

The sound hole in a stringed instrument like a guitar or violin improves the tone. It also makes the music louder so your family can hear it throughout the house.

A hole can be mysterious . . .

If you happen to get an invitation to a picnic on Neptune tomorrow, a wormhole—a tunnel across time and space—could get you there in plenty of time. But nobody knows if wormholes exist outside of science fiction. They were predicted by Einstein's theory of general relativity but have not been detected yet. Better send your regrets to Neptune, at least for now.

. . . or annoyingly familiar.

You may not be able to travel through a wormhole, and your socks may still be intact. But there are holes all around you, and they are really something! Big or small, troubling or useful, strange or commonplace—life without them would be a whole other story.

ENGLISH IS FULL OF HOLES

When it comes to talking about holes, people have gotten creative. Some words and phrases in English that were first used to label physical holes are now also used to communicate other concepts. Check out these examples and try them in conversation sometime!

Castles had narrow slits to let in light and for archers to shoot arrows at an enemy without being a visible target themselves. Today, the term for such an opening, **loophole**, refers to a gap in a rule or law that technically allows you to do something that was meant to be forbidden. This kid found a loophole in the "pants required at the dinner table" rule.

People who kept pigeons—to carry messages, for example—built sets of little box-shaped holes where the birds slept and took shelter from the rain. Someone who is **pigeonholed** isn't crammed in an actual bird box, but the idea of that tight space is still at play. They're being defined by others as belonging to a narrow category or having only one interest or skill, when of course everyone is multifaceted.

If you get a golf ball into the hole with just one swing—rather than a bunch of hits and a potential detour into a sandpit—that's a **hole in one**. But you can also use the same phrase if a different impressive thing is accomplished on the first try. Regardless of whether there was an actual golf ball involved or you just correctly spelled a fifteen-letter word you'd never heard before, your hole in one probably deserves a high five.

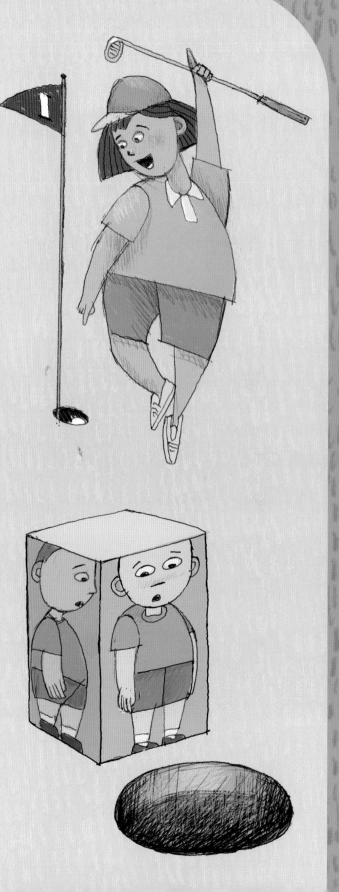

Have you ever tried to **poke holes** in your parents' reasoning? If you think their argument—about why you can't stay up late or fill a room entirely with popcorn, for example—is **full of holes**, you might point out all the ways it's not supported by evidence or logic. It's like they're presenting their argument as if it's a bucket of water, and you're demonstrating it's actually a sieve.

A toddler—or a big kid, for that matter—wouldn't have much luck getting a square peg into a round hole in their shape-sorting toy. Similarly, someone who feels like a **square peg in a round hole** is in a situation where they think they don't quite fit in.

Hole up can mean hiding from danger in a cave or other protected space. But you can also say you're going to hole up somewhere in order to focus on something, like finishing a great book without being disturbed.

If someone says you've **dug yourself into a hole**, you've gotten yourself into a pretty awkward situation through your own actions. Every time you try to explain, you somehow make it worse—digging that metaphorical hole deeper. Someone might tell you to "stop digging," meaning you need to change your strategy if you want to get out of trouble.

Author Lewis Carroll gave us the phrase **down the rabbit hole** in his 1865 book *Alice's Adventures in Wonderland*, in which Alice fell down the White Rabbit's hole and found herself in a strange new world. "Going down a rabbit hole" is now widely used to mean digging for more and more information on a fascinating topic. (After reading this book, you may have to tell your friends you went down a rabbit hole learning about holes.)

THIS HOLE IS NOT REALLY A HOLE

Have you ever heard someone say their room—or maybe their purse or their backpack—is a **black hole**? They mean things seem to disappear in there with little hope of finding them. The term was made up by an astronomer to describe something that really happens in outer space. A black hole forms when a very large star—larger than our own Sun—burns up its fuel and implodes, leaving behind a tiny point. That point is so dense and heavy that its gravitational pull even gobbles up light! A black hole is not actually a true hole. But being a zone of super intense gravity is still pretty cool. Scientists first saw black holes in 1971 using an X-ray telescope, and they managed to take the first photo of the black hole in the middle of our Milky Way galaxy in 2022.

FURTHER READING

Davies, Monika. *How Far Underground? Burrowing Animals.* Mankato, MN: Amicus Ink, 2018.

DeCristofano, Carolyn Cinami. *A Black Hole Is Not a Hole.* Watertown, MA: Charlesbridge, 2021.

"Deep Thoughts Blog: Exploring Blue Holes," MOTE Marine Laboratory and Aquarium.
mote.org/research/program/benthic-ecology/deep-thoughts-blog

"Molluscs: Moon Snail Preys on Cockles," Shape of Life.
www.shapeoflife.org/video/molluscs-moon-snail-preys-cockles

"Ozone," NASA Science Space Place. *spaceplace.nasa.gov/search/ozone*

"The Ozone Hole: We Need More Sunscreen," EO Kids, NASA Earth Observatory.
earthobservatory.nasa.gov/blogs/eokids/the-ozone-hole-we-need-more-sunscreen

"Pinhole Camera," National Geographic Kids.
kids.nationalgeographic.com/explore/books/pinhole-camera

Rusch, Elizabeth. *Mario and the Hole in the Sky: How a Chemist Saved Our Planet.*
Watertown, MA: Charlesbridge, 2019.

"Sinkholes," USGS Water Science School, June 9, 2018.
usgs.gov/special-topic/water-science-school/science/sinkholes

Stewart, Melissa. *Tree Hole Homes: Daytime Dens and Nighttime Nooks.*
New York: Random House, 2022.